QUIZ BOOK
2017

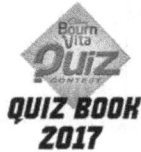

Derek O'Brien was born in Kolkata. He began his career as a journalist for *Sportsworld* magazine but soon shifted to advertising. After working for a number of very successful years as Creative Head of Oglivy, Derek decided to focus all his energy and talent in his passion—quizzing.

Today, Derek is Asia's best-known quizmaster and the CEO of Derek O'Brien & Associates. He is the host of the longest-running game show on Indian television, the Cadbury Bournvita Quiz Contest, for which he was voted the Best Anchor of a Game Show at the Indian Television Academy Awards for three years in a row. Always innovating, Derek is also credited with having conducted the first quiz on Twitter in 2010.

Derek has written over fifty bestselling reference, quiz and textbooks. In 2011, he was voted to the Rajya Sabha as a Member of Parliament (MP) and is the Leader of the Trinamool Congress Parliamentary Party in the Rajya Sabha.

Keep in touch with Derek on Twitter, where his handle is @quizderek.

Other books by Derek O'Brien
(published by Rupa Publications)

Bournvita Quiz Contest Quiz Book 2012

The Ultimate BQC Book of Knowledge (Volumes 1 and 2)

The Best of BQC

Derek's Challenge

*Speak Up, Speak Out: My Favourite Elocution Pieces and
How to Deliver Them*

My Way: Success Mantras of 12 Achievers

Derek Introduces: 100 Iconic Indians

Bournvita Quiz Contest Quiz Book 2014

BQC Quiz Book 3

QUIZ BOOK
2017

DEREK O'BRIEN

RUPA

Published by
Rupa Publications India Pvt. Ltd 2017
7/16, Ansari Road, Daryaganj
New Delhi 110002

Sales Centres:
Allahabad Bengaluru Chennai
Hyderabad Jaipur Kathmandu
Kolkata Mumbai

Copyright © Derek O'Brien & Associates 2017

ISBN: 978-81-291-4531-4

First impression 2017

10 9 8 7 6 5 4 3 2 1

The moral right of the author has been asserted.

Printed at Repro Knowledgecast Limited, India

HALL OF FAME

PAST WINNERS OF THE BOURNVITA
QUIZ CONTEST

1994-1995, Mumbai

Campion High School, Mumbai
Balakrishnan Sivaraman, Sudhanshu Bhuwalka

1995-1996, Mumbai

Kendriya Vidyalaya, Powai, Mumbai
Eipy Koshy, Gourav Shah

1996-1997, Mumbai

Bombay International High School, Mumbai
Nirica Borges, Advait Behara

1997, Mumbai

Mount Saint Mary's School, New Delhi
Joe Christy, Maninder Singh Jessel

1997-1998, Mumbai

Bombay Scottish High School, Mumbai
Shaambhavi Pandyaa, Rahul Lalmalani

1998, Mumbai

Sacred Heart Convent School, Jamshedpur
Ela Verma, Lavanya Raghavan

1998-1999, Mumbai

Indian School Al Ghubra, Muscat
Anand Raghavan, Hitesh Kanvatirtha

1999, Mumbai

Maneckji Cooper High School, Mumbai
Ipsita Bandopadhyay, Gourav Bhattacharya

1999-2000, Mumbai

Chettinad Vidyashram, Chennai
Siddharth, Karthik Das

2000-2001, Mumbai

Bharatiya Vidya Bhavan, Hyderabad
Ananya Bhaskar, Aksha Anand

2001 September, Mumbai

Brightlands, Dehradun
Ankur Bharadwaj, Shray Sharma

2001 December, Mumbai

Little Flower High School, Hyderabad
G. Mithilesh, K Siddharth Reddy

2002 February, Bentota, Sri Lanka

G.D. Birla Centre For Education, Kolkata
Namrata Basu, Rituparna Dey

2002 June, Mumbai

Kerala Samajam Public School, Jamshedpur
Saurav Biswas, Kunal Mohan

2002 September, Mumbai

Jamnabai Narsee School, Mumbai

Sharan Narayanan, Vishnu Shrest

2003 January, Kerala

Naval Public High School, Mumbai

Apoorva Sharma, Abhishek Pandit

2003 May, Kolkata

St. Patrick's Higher Secondary School, Asansol

Pushpen Dasgupta, Shamik Ray

2003 October, Sangla

St. Agnes Loreto Day School, Lucknow

Aastha Srivastava, Illa Gupta

2004 February, Swabhumi, Kolkata

Apeejay School, Jalandhar

Mohit Thukral, Sahil Sareen

2004 May, Goa

Springdales School, Delhi

Anirudh Sridhar, B. Anuraag

2004 July, Indian Military Academy, Dehradun

The Mother's International School, Delhi

Krittika Adhikary, Milind Ganjoo

2004 November, Kolkata

Amity International, New Delhi

Aishwarya Singhal, Adarsh Modi

2005 August, Kolkata
Amity International, New Delhi
Utkarsh Johari, Aishwarya Singhal

2006 July, Kolkata
Riverdale High School, Dehradun
Kartikeya Panwar, Sumit Nair

2006 November, Kolkata
Seth Jaipuria School, Lucknow
Ratnaksha Lele, Ananya Kumar Singh

2011 August, Kolkata
Amity International School, Noida
Kripi Badonia, Shinjini Biswas

2012 January, Kolkata
Birla Vidya Niketan, New Delhi
Anusha Malhotra, Nitya Bansal

2013 January, Kolkata
Vidyaniketan Public School (Ullal), Bengaluru
Shashank Niranjan Gowda, Mainak Mandal

2014 December, Kolkata
Centre Point, Amravati Road, Nagpur
Ratnasambhav Sahu, Tanaya Ramani

2016 January, Shantiniketan
Brightlands, Dehradun
Arhaan Ahmad, Vishwas Chawla

SET 1

TAKE YOUR PICK

1. Corbetti, Jacksoni and Sumatran are the subspecies of which animal?
   A. Tiger
   B. Snake
   C. Spider
   D. Zebra

2. Which of these words can you type using the letters on one row of a QWERTY keyboard?
   A. PORTRAIT
   B. TYPEWRITER
   C. WEREWOLF
   D. ELEPHANT

3. In which of these forts would you find the Qal'a-i-Kuhna-Masjid?
   A. Agra Fort
   B. Red Fort
   C. Golconda Fort
   D. Purana Qila

4. Who wrote *The Chimes, The Battle of Life: A Love Story* and *The Haunted Man and the Ghost's Bargain*?
   A. Mark Twain

    B. Charles Dickens

    C. Victor Hugo

    D. Thomas Hardy

5. Which of these is not a type of trouser?
    A. Bell-bottoms
    B. Cargos
    C. Tuxedos
    D. Jeans

6. Pierre de Coubertin, a founding member of the International Olympic Committee, is buried in Switzerland. In which country is his heart interred?
    A. Germany
    B. Italy
    C. Greece
    D. France

7. In which part of the human body are the two small muscles tensor tympani and stapedius located?
    A. Eyes
    B. Ears
    C. Nose
    D. Wrist

8. To which list has India contributed names like Agni, Akash, Bijli, Jal, Lehar, Megh, and Bangladesh has contributed Onil, Ogni, Nisha, Giri?
    A. Submarines
    B. Tropical cyclones
    C. Trains connecting India and Bangladesh

D. Species of tigers

9. What is located on 1st Avenue between 42nd and 48th Street in New York City?
   A. UN headquaters
   B. White House
   C. Statue of Liberty
   D. Google headquarters

10. According to legend, what first arrived in Pampore in Jammu and Kashmir when two Sufi saints, Khwaja Masood Wali and Hazrat Sheikh Shariffudin, rewarded a local chief with a flower bulb?
    A. Saffron
    B. Clove
    C. Pepper
    D. Cardamom

11. How many ten thousands will make a million?
    A. 10
    B. 100
    C. 1,000
    D. 10,000

12. Which famous comic-strip series features the fictional countries of Syldavia and Borduria?
    A. Garfield
    B. Calvin and Hobbes
    C. The Adventures of Tintin
    D. The Adventures of Asterix

13. Who composed the music for the 2010 film *127 Hours*?
    A. Ilaiyaraaja
    B. Jay Z
    C. A.R. Rahman
    D. Pritam

14. According to the 2011 census, if Uttar Pradesh has the highest population in India, which state has the second highest?
    A. Maharashtra
    B. Bihar
    C. Tamil Nadu
    D. Odisha

15. The recipient of which of these awards gets a bronze statue of Vagdevi (Saraswati)?
    A. Bharat Ratna
    B. Sahitya Akademi Award
    C. Jnanpith Award
    D. Arjuna Award

BUZZER

1. Which landmark was built earlier: Charminar or Taj Mahal?
2. Which animal initially feeds a predigested eucalyptus called pap to its babies?
3. Which celestial body had its last visitor on 11 December 1972?
4. Which union territory in India has only 36 islands

contrary to the meaning of its name?

5. In which fictional town can you find the Madras Daily Messenger's office, the Ishwara Temple and the Welcome Restaurant?

6. Which team won the 2015 edition of the IPL?

7. The word phablet comes from the words tablet and...

8. Which Mughal emperor defeated Hem Chandra Vikramaditya on 5 November 1556?

SET-2

TAKE YOUR PICK

1. Honeybees live in colonies generally consisting of drones, workers, and a...
   A. King
   B. Queen
   C. Prince
   D. Bishop

2. The First Battalion of the Somerset Light Infantry was...
   A. Raised to conduct the first census in India
   B. The last British troop to leave independent India
   C. The troop that took the Kohinoor to the Queen
   D. Sent to India to dismantle the Taj Mahal

3. Which fabric, originating in Iraq, was so fine that the Egyptian pharaohs are said to have used them for wrapping mummies?
   A. Muslin
   B. Calico
   C. Chiffon
   D. Brocade

4. Marie Curie named polonium, a chemical element discovered by her, after her...
    A. Favourite sport
    B. Daughter
    C. Native country
    D. Teacher

5. Which cartoon character says, 'Khaali pet dimaag ki batti nahin jalti'?
    A. Motu
    B. Mighty Raju
    C. Chhota Bheem
    D. Arjun

6. Which of these teams was not a part of the inaugural season of the IPL?
    A. Mumbai Indians
    B. Delhi Daredevils
    C. Gujarat Lions
    D. Kolkata Knight Riders

7. Which organ of the human body goes through a period of relaxation called diastole and a period of contraction called systole?
    A. Heart
    B. Liver
    C. Kidney
    D. Lung

8. Who is considered to be the 'Father of Leap Year' and credited for introducing the concept?

    A. Caligula
    B. Nero
    C. Horatio Nelson
    D. Julius Caesar

9. If thumbs up denotes 'like' on Facebook, which of the following is its equivalent on Instagram?
    A. Sun
    B. Smiley
    C. Heart
    D. Star

10. The colour and shape of the white variety of the fruit of which plant is the source of its common name?
    A. Beetroot
    B. Radish
    C. Eggplant
    D. Pumpkin

11. Which of these waterbodies contains some of the hottest and saltiest seawater in the world?
    A. Red Sea
    B. Black Sea
    C. Yellow Sea
    D. Arabian Sea

12. In the *Ramayana*, who was Lakshmana's mother?
    A. Kaikeyi
    B. Kaushalya
    C. Sumitra
    D. Sita

13. The red colour on the flag of NCC stands for...
    A. The sun
    B. The Indian Army
    C. Martyrs of India
    D. Fire

14. Which Nobel Laureate's house in Dummerston, Vermont is named Naulakha, after a novel written by him and Wolcott Balestier?
    A. Rabindranath Tagore
    B. Rudyard Kipling
    C. V.S. Naipaul
    D. Samuel Beckett

15. Putul Nautch is the traditional rod puppet form of which state of India?
    A. Kerala
    B. Haryana
    C. West Bengal
    D. Tamil Nadu

BUZZER

1. Spiders are insects: true or false?
2. The name of which state of India begins with 'And'?
3. The train Andaman Express connects New Delhi to Andaman Islands: serious or joking?
4. Which fibre is produced by the insect *Antheraea assamensis*?
5. Which historical character got a diary on her thirteenth birthday and wrote letters to an imaginary

girlfriend named Kitty?
6. The founder of which religion had an elder sister named Bebe Nanki?
7. What is the national sport of Bangladesh?
8. A gastroenterologist specializes in treating the diseases of the stomach or heart?

SET-3

TAKE YOUR PICK

1. What did Carl Wilhelm Scheele call 'fire air' because it supported combustion?
   A. Nitrogen
   B. Oxygen
   C. Helium
   D. Chlorine

2. Where did the Great Dane canine breed originate?
   A. Denmark
   B. Italy
   C. France
   D. Germany

3. Australia broke which country's record in 2015, when it scored 417 runs to become the highest scorer in an ICC Cricket World Cup Match? ?
   A. India
   B. Sri Lanka
   C. West Indies
   D. England

4. In which UNESCO World Heritage Site complex would you find the Salimgarh Fort?

A. Red Fort
B. Agra Fort
C. Taj Mahal
D. Humayun's Tomb

5. After reading which of author Charles Lutwidge Dodgson's books did Queen Victoria request him to dedicate his next book to her?
A. *David Copperfield*
B. *Alice's Adventures in Wonderland*
C. *Far From the Madding Crowd*
D. *Around the World in Eighty Days*

6. In 1973, Bhutan issued one of these, which had the ability to play their national anthem. In 2013, Belgium issued one of these, which smelt and tasted like chocolate. What is being talked about here?
A. Stamps
B. Banknotes
C. Flags
D. Coins

7. Motu, from the animated series *Motu Patlu*, loves to eat...
A. Laddoos
B. Samosas
C. Dhoklas
D. Rasgullas

8. Which symbol did Ray Tomlinson call 'the only preposition on the keyboard'?

A. @
B. &
C. $
D. %

9. Complete this quote by Pliny: '_____ is the most valuable, not only of precious stones, but of all things in this world.'
   A. Opal
   B. Diamond
   C. Ruby
   D. Sapphire

10. According to the India State of Forest Report 2015, which state has the largest forest cover in terms of area?
    A. Kerala
    B. Odisha
    C. Madhya Pradesh
    D. Manipur

11. The word 'Mulligatawny' in the name of the soup comes from the Tamil word for...
    A. Cardamom
    B. Turmeric
    C. Tamarind
    D. Pepper

12. Which of these is a type of loose-fitting pants?
    A. Poncho
    B. Palazzo

    C. Sombrero
    D. Fez

13. In which part of the body would you find cells called osteoclasts and osteocytes?
    A. Bones
    B. Hair
    C. Blood
    D. Muscles

14. In which film would you meet the characters named Zazu, Rafiki and Sarabi?
    A. *Inside Out*
    B. *Finding Nemo*
    C. *Shrek*
    D. *The Lion King*

15. What do the number of dots on all six faces of a dice add up to?
    A. 27
    B. 25
    C. 21
    D. 34

BUZZER

1. In which country is the medieval palace complex of Gorkha located?
2. Red kangaroos are herbivores or carnivores?
3. In which cartoon series would you meet characters named Nobita and Shizuka?

4. In 2015, which country became the world's largest producer of potatoes?
5. In English, the name of which state of India has the maximum number of letters in it?
6. In cricket, what is the 22-yard strip of ground between the two sets of stumps called?
7. Which Mughal emperor was Aurangzeb's grandfather?
8. Which city in Rajasthan is called the Blue City for its indigo or blue-coloured buildings?

SET-4

TAKE YOUR PICK

1. What does one clean with a dentifrice?
   A. Shoes
   B. Spectacles
   C. Nails
   D. Teeth

2. In 1903, the photo of which historic moment was taken by John T. Daniels, an attendant from the local life-saving station?
   A. First flight by man
   B. First ascent of Mount Everest
   C. Man landing on the Moon
   D. First kidney transplant

3. Who wrote all the songs for A.R. Rahman's 2014 album *Raunaq*?
   A. Arun Jaitley
   B. Kapil Sibal
   C. Sushma Swaraj
   D. Rahul Gandhi

4. The European exploration of which UNESCO World Heritage Site began when Captain James Cook ran his

ship aground on it?
A. The Sundarbans
B. Great Barrier Reef
C. Venice
D. Kakadu National Park

5. Queen Alexandra's Birdwing is one of the largest
   species of...
   A. Albatross
   B. Butterfly
   C. Flamingo
   D. Dragonfly

6. In 1953, John Hunt, a British army officer born in
   India led a team to successfully achieve which feat?
   A. Climb Mount Everest
   B. Win the first Olympic medal for India
   C. Conduct the first general elections in India
   D. Do the first heart transplant

7. After which Indian is the minor planet (4538), located
   roughly between the orbits of Mars and Jupiter,
   named?
   A. Saina Nehwal
   B. Sania Mirza
   C. Vishwanathan Anand
   D. M.S. Dhoni

8. Which word is described in the dictionary as 'send an
   email or text message'?
   A. Ping

    B. Poke
    C. Like
    D. Click

9. Rampur, Sitapur and Chitrakoot are districts in which state of India?
    A. Maharashtra
    B. Karnataka
    C. Uttar Pradesh
    D. Odisha

10. In India, 28 February is celebrated as the National Science Day to mark the achievements of which famous Indian?
    A. Vikram Sarabhai
    B. S. Ramanujan
    C. S.N. Bose
    D. C.V. Raman

11. *The Comedy of Errors* is the shortest play by which author?
    A. William Shakespeare
    B. Charles Dickens
    C. Mark Twain
    D. Jane Austen

12. What does the Pyruvate Scale measure?
    A. Pungency in garlic and onions
    B. Speed of wind
    C. Blood pressure
    D. 'Hotness' of chillies

13. Which small shrub, commonly cultivated for its dye, is also known as Egyptian privet, Jamaica mignonette or Reseda?
    A. Saffron
    B. Indigo
    C. Henna
    D. Turmeric

14. Which disease is named after a river in Africa where the virus was first identified in 1976?
    A. Zika
    B. Ebola
    C. Chikungunya
    D. Dengue

15. Which of these union territories is represented in the Rajya Sabha?
    A. Delhi
    B. Chandigarh
    C. Lakshadweep
    D. Andaman and Nicobar Islands

BUZZER

1. Which number connects the rings on the Olympic flag and the vowels in the English alphabet?
2. Which 2015 film, starring Anushka Sharma, shares its name with a national highway in India?
3. In Japan, which mountain is one of the Three Holy Mountains, along with Mount Tate and Mount Haku?
4. Which landmark is located in a state capital: the

Golden Temple or the Hawa Mahal?

5. The International Indian Film Academy (IIFA) Awards have never been held in India. Serious or Joking?

6. The name of which state in India starts with the first consonant of the alphabet?

7. What does the 'S' in the organization ISRO stand for?

8. *Prem Pachisi* and *Prem Battisi* are works of which famous author?

SET-5

TAKE YOUR PICK

1. Who left his Nobel Prize award money to his wife in 1919 even before he won it in 1921?
   A. C.V. Raman
   B. Albert Einstein
   C. William Roentgen
   D. Pierre Curie

2. Winston Churchill became an honorary citizen of the US in 1963. Who became the country's honorary citizen in 1996?
   A. Jimmy Carter
   B. The Dalai Lama
   C. Mother Teresa
   D. Nelson Mandela

3. The Chinese name for which fiery-coloured animal is hun-ho, meaning fire fox?
   A. Red panda
   B. Firefly
   C. Ruby-throated hummingbird
   D. Greater flamingo

4. In which category has the Nobel Prize been awarded the least number of times?
   A. Economics
   B. Literature
   C. Medicine
   D. Physics

5. In the history of the men's FIFA World Cup, which is the only team to have played in every tournament?
   A. Italy
   B. Brazil
   C. Argentina
   D. Uruguay

6. The building of the Supreme Court of India is shaped like…
   A. A balance
   B. A hammer
   C. A pen
   D. A chariot

7. The green-coloured enemies in which game were inspired by the 2009 epidemic of swine flu?
   A. Temple Run
   B. Angry Birds
   C. Pokīmon
   D. Dark Souls

8. Which waterbody is called Darya-ye Khezer in Persian?
   A. Red Sea
   B. Yellow Sea

C. Caspian Sea
D. Mediterranean Sea

9. The word for 'a small piece of partly burnt coal or wood that has stopped giving off flames' gave the name to which fairy-tale character?
   A. Thumbelina
   B. Gretel
   C. Rapunzel
   D. Cinderella

10. Who is the president of The Indian Red Cross Society?
    A. The President of India
    B. The Union Minister of Health
    C. The Prime Minister
    D. The Chief Justice of India

11. What do we call the pasta that comes in the form of long slender threads?
    A. Vermicelli
    B. Penne
    C. Lasagne
    D. Fusilli

12. The motifs of the triple bird and the seated Buddha, used in Paithani saris, are influenced by which UNESCO World Heritage Site?
    A. Taj Mahal
    B. Ajanta Caves
    C. Red Fort

D. Agra Fort

13. The last-known natural case of which disease occurred in Somalia in 1977?
    A. Smallpox
    B. Rabies
    C. Measles
    D. Malaria

14. Which Indian leader was cremated at Girgaum Chowpatty, which has now been renamed as Swaraj Bhoomi?
    A. Bal Gangadhar Tilak
    B. Lal Bahadur Shastri
    C. Bipin Chandra Pal
    D. Lala Lajpat Rai

15. In the *Ramayana*, who was also known as Vaideha and Maithila?
    A. Janak
    B. Dashratha
    C. Ravana
    D. Lakshmana

BUZZER

1. Before 1 November 2000, Chhattisgarh was a part of which Indian state?
2. What is described in a dictionary as 'an Indian sweet made of a coil of batter fried and steeped in syrup'?
3. The first Shatabdi Express ran from Delhi to which

historic place in Uttar Pradesh?
4. Which sound made by a dog would also be of interest to a botanist?
5. Which sporting equipment is sometimes referred to as a 'birdie'?
6. The first model of which device, used with a computer, was a 3 x 4 x 3-inch block of wood on two wheels?
7. In the human body, the nape is the back of your neck or stomach?
8. In a dictionary, which month of the Gregorian calendar will appear between July and March?

TAKE YOUR PICK

1. In 2012, which monument was given a bath for the first time in the 213 years of its existence?
    A. Taj Mahal
    B. Gol Gumbaz
    C. Hawa Mahal
    D. Red Fort

2. Which is the largest country in the world composed solely of islands?
    A. Japan
    B. Indonesia
    C. Greenland
    D. Australia

3. Who was the first sitting member of the Rajya Sabha to receive the Bharat Ratna?
    A. Atal Bihari Vajpayee
    B. Indira Gandhi
    C. Lata Mangeshkar
    D. Sachin Tendulkar

4. The name of which part of a building comes from the Latin word which means 'to run'?
    A. Corridor

   B. Verandah
   C. Lobby
   D. Window

5. If you were eating xacuti, prawn balchao or bebinca, which state would you be in?
   A. Tripura
   B. Gujarat
   C. Himachal Pradesh
   D. Goa

6. What does an emperor penguin normally keep in a 'brood pouch'?
   A. Fish
   B. Snowflakes
   C. Eggs
   D. Stones

7. The Kilikili language, with 750 words and 40 rules of grammar, was created for which film?
   A. *The Lord of the Rings*
   B. *Avatar*
   C. *Baahubali*
   D. *Bajrangi Bhaijaan*

8. Which emoji was adjudged the Oxford Dictionaries Word of the Year in 2015?
   A. Tears of joy
   B. Smiling with sunglasses
   C. Thinking face
   D. Winking

9. Who won the Nobel Prize for physics in the year Karl Landsteiner won it for medicine?
   A. Albert Einstein
   B. C.V. Raman
   C. Niels Bohr
   D. Guglielmo Marconi

10. Loafer, pump and wedge are all types of...
    A. Hats
    B. Shoes
    C. Umbrellas
    D. Jackets

11. With which of these is the term olfactory associated?
    A. Vision
    B. Smell
    C. Touch
    D. Hearing

12. The name of the Indian folk dance 'garba' comes from a Sanskrit word meaning...
    A. Incense sticks
    B. Lamp inside a pot
    C. Spiral movement
    D. Garland

13. How many ₹5 coins do you need to make ₹2 lakh?
    A. 4,000
    B. 40,000
    C. 4 lakh
    D. 40 lakh

14. Pomiculture refers to…
    A. Breeding of fish
    B. Fruit growing
    C. Pearl farming
    D. Cattle rearing

15. In 2010, the UN declared whose seventy-ninth birth anniversary as World Students' Day?
    A. Dr S. Radhakrishnan
    B. Swami Vivekananda
    C. A.P.J Abdul Kalam
    D. Nelson Mandela

BUZZER

1. *Capsicum frutescens* is a variety of which spice: chilli or mustard?
2. Russia, the largest country in the world, has a higher population than Bangladesh: serious or joking?
3. In 2015, who became the first Indian woman to reach the finals of the All England Open Badminton Championships?
4. Tian Han wrote the national anthem of which country?
5. People in Belgium speak Belgian: true or false?
6. Which is the first film in which Aamir Khan has played a double role?
7. Name the city founded by Maharaj Suraj Sen in honour of Sage Gwalipa.
8. The Old English word from which 'fortnight' is derived refers to how many nights?

TAKE YOUR PICK

1. Who wrote *Serve to Win: The 14-Day Gluten-Free Plan for Physical and Mental Excellence*?
   A. Sanjeev Kapoor
   B. Novak Djokovic
   C. Roger Federer
   D. Viswanathan Anand

2. Where would you come across landmarks called Yellow Band and Geneva Spur?
   A. Mount Everest
   B. The Sahara Desert
   C. The Moon
   D. Antarctica

3. Who among these wrote the first volume of their autobiography in the Landsberg am Lech fortress?
   A. Nelson Mandela
   B. Anne Frank
   C. Adolf Hitler
   D. Benito Mussolini

4. Seals, walruses and sea lions belong to the order called Pinnipedia. What does Pinnipedia mean?

A. Long-tooth
B. Wing-foot
C. Hairy-one
D. Soft-skin

5. Agrifound Dark Red and Agrifound White are different varieties of what?
   A. Apples
   B. Onions
   C. Beetroots
   D. Cherries

6. *The Force Awakens* is the advertising line of which movie franchise?
   A. *Star Wars*
   B. *Avengers*
   C. *Mission Impossible*
   D. *Ant-Man*

7. The 'woofer' and the 'tweeter' are different types of...
   A. Dogs
   B. Pianos
   C. Loudspeakers
   D. Birds

8. What is used in large amounts to clear snow off the streets?
   A. Water
   B. Salt
   C. Vinegar
   D. Pepper

9. Which of these languages does not appear in the Eighth Schedule of the Constitution of India?
    A. Sindhi
    B. Bodo
    C. Bhojpuri
    D. Nepali

10. What started on 12 March 1930 and lasted for twenty-four days?
    A. The Census of India
    B. The Maha Kumbh Mela
    C. The Dandi March
    D. The first Asian Games

11. Which was the first item from Assam to obtain the Geographical Indications tag?
    A. Bhut Jolokia chillies
    B. Assam tea
    C. Muga silk
    D. Joha rice

12. *The Bachelor of Arts* was R.K. Narayan's second novel. Which was his first?
    A. *Malgudi Days*
    B. *The Man-Eater of Malgudi*
    C. *Swami and Friends*
    D. *The Guide*

13. According to legend, what was created when the pakhawaj accidentally split into two parts?
    A. The ghatam

B. The dholak
C. The tabla
D. The nagara

14. Which of these elements is named after a Swedish city?
    A. Strontium
    B. Holmium
    C. Berkelium
    D. Polonium

15. Who was the Government of India's cabinet minister of finance from 1982–4?
    A. P. Chidambaram
    B. Manmohan Singh
    C. Pranab Mukherjee
    D. Yashwant Sinha

BUZZER

1. Which is Pakistan's national mountain?
2. In Indian Railways, which quota is abbreviated as DF?
3. The Mahatma Gandhi-Nelson Mandela cricket series is played between India and...
4. What constitutes about 90 per cent of a cucumber by weight?
5. What is the name of the alien mineral that can deprive Superman of his powers?
6. Which singer topped the June 2015 'Most Followed Celebrities on Twitter' list released by *Forbes*?
7. In a dictionary, which day of the week will come

between Thursday and Wednesday?

8. Rainbow hedgehog and artichoke or obregnita are different species of which plant?

SET-8

TAKE YOUR PICK

1. Who initiated the import of silk cocoons from China to encourage silk rearing in Mysore (now Mysuru)?
   A. Raja Raja Chola I
   B. Krishna Deva Raya
   C. Tipu Sultan
   D. Shah Jahan

2. Which is the only big cat that can turn in mid-air while following its prey?
   A. The lion
   B. The leopard
   C. The cheetah
   D. The jaguar

3. Whose celebratory stance is called the 'To Di World' pose?
   A. Cristiano Ronaldo
   B. Usain Bolt
   C. Roger Federer
   D. Michael Phelps

4. As it takes less fuel to launch a spacecraft in lower gravity, most bases are located near the...

    A. Tropic of Cancer
    B. Equator
    C. South Pole
    D. Prime Meridian

5. In 1903–4, what appeared on the first machine-struck coins of Hyderabad?
    A. The Salar Jung Museum
    B. The Charminar
    C. The Falaknuma Palace
    D. A pearl

6. Which is the national heritage animal of India?
    A. The Asiatic lion
    B. The elephant
    C. The one-horned rhinoceros
    D. The nilgai

7. Bridge, temple and nose pads are parts of which of these objects?
    A. Umbrella
    B. Eyeglasses
    C. Books
    D. Cricket bats

8. *Road Song of the Bandar-Log* and *Hunting Song of the Seeonee Pack*. These are chapters of…
    A. *Tarzan of the Apes*
    B. *Black Beauty*
    C. *The Jungle Book*
    D. *Moby-Dick*

9. The name of which of these food items comes from a Turkish word meaning 'turn or rotate'?
   A. Shaslik
   B. Shawarma
   C. Kebab
   D. Paratha

10. Around AD 1777, Nanak Shahis were issued in Amritsar. What were these?
    A. Books
    B. Coins
    C. Dhotis
    D. Turbans

11. Who published his telescopic observations in a paper called *The Starry Messenger*?
    A. Mark Zuckerberg
    B. Galileo Galilei
    C. Steve Jobs
    D. Julius Caesar

12. What is the session of the Indian Parliament from February to April–May called?
    A. The Budget Session
    B. The Monsoon Session
    C. The Summer Session
    D. The Joint Session

13. In mythology, who was the ninth of the ten incarnations of Vishnu?
    A. Krishna

    B. Rama

    C. Matsya

    D. Vamana

14. First detected in 2009, which infection was so named because the virus was similar to those found in pigs?
    A. Dengue
    B. Swine Flu
    C. Chicken Pox
    D. Zika

15. Which historical character did Ranveer Singh play in a 2015 film starring Priyanka Chopra?
    A. Ashoka
    B. Alexander
    C. Akbar
    D. Peshwa Bajirao

BUZZER

1. Jaisalmer is the largest district of which state of India?
2. Lupus nephritis is the inflammation of which organ of the human body?
3. Which cricketer his first ODI hundred in his seventy-ninth match?
4. 144 square inches is equal to one square foot: true or false?
5. Which part of the human eye gets its name from a Greek word which means 'rainbow'?
6. Who was also known as Shakyamuni: Buddha or Mahavira?

7. Jane Goodall is famous for her research on cheetahs or chimpanzees?
8. What does A in the acronym NATO stand for?

SET-9

1. Which city was founded by the fifth king of the Qutb Shahi dynasty?
   A. Bengaluru
   B. Hyderabad
   C. Lucknow
   D. Ajmer

2. Which father-son duo appeared together on-screen for the first time in the film *Shandaar*?
   A. Rishi and Ranbir Kapoor
   B. Pankaj and Shahid Kapur
   C. Jackie and Tiger Shroff
   D. Boney and Arjun Kapoor

3. After thirty-six years, Indian women participated in which team sport at the 2016 Olympic Games?
   A. Field hockey
   B. Football
   C. Gymnastics
   D. Volleyball

4. Narwhal is a species of...
   A. Seal

B. Whale
C. Deer
D. Penguin

5. Pang Lhabsol is celebrated in honour of which presiding deity of Sikkim?
   A. K2
   B. Kanchenjunga
   C. Mount Everest
   D. Lhotse

6. In which UNESCO World Heritage Site would you find the tombs of Akbarabadi Begum and Fatehpuri Begum, the builder's wives?
   A. Taj Mahal
   B. Humayun's Tomb
   C. Red Fort
   D. Charminar

7. In the Preamble to the Constitution of India, what comes between the words sovereign and secular?
   A. Autocratic
   B. Socialist
   C. Republic
   D. Capitalist

8. What are brown, castor and icing different kinds of?
   A. Sugar
   B. Salt
   C. Honey
   D. Pepper

9. In which of these books would you meet the Frog Footman and the Mock Turtle?
   A. *Alice's Adventures in Wonderland*
   B. *Black Beauty*
   C. *Animal Farm*
   D. *David Copperfield*

10. Who is the chancellor of the Visva-Bharati University?
    A. The President of India
    B. The Prime Minister of India
    C. The Chief Minister of West Bengal
    D. The Governor of West Bengal

11. In which category has the Nobel Prize been awarded the most number of times?
    A. Physics
    B. Peace
    C. Medicine
    D. Literature

12. Tongue, insole and stud are parts of a…
    A. Shoe
    B. Shirt
    C. Umbrella
    D. Fan

13. Before 1972, what was the national animal of India?
    A. The elephant
    B. The lion
    C. The one-horned rhinocerous
    D. The tiger

14. In the Mahabharata, after the war, Yudhisthira was crowned the king of which of these places?
    A. Dwarka
    B. Hastinapura
    C. Mathura
    D. Ayodhya

15. This element, known as Argentum in Latin, is widely used in the form of leaf or a foil called varak for decorating sweets. Which element am I talking about?
    A. Aluminium
    B. Silver
    C. Iron
    D. Copper

BUZZER

1. The name Indonesia comes from two Greek words meaning 'India' and...
2. Fazli, Gulabkhas and Amrapalli are varieties of which fruit: apple, mango or banana?
3. Which team does Moeen Ali represent in international cricket: England or Bangladesh?
4. Who made his acting debut in *Biwi Ho To Aisi* where he played a supporting role?
5. Only the male Anopheles mosquito can spread malaria: serious or joking?
6. In India, what did we have earlier: a woman prime minister or a woman president?

7. The name of which Indian state means 'Land of Coconuts' in the native language?

8. Connect a Marvel comic character trained at the Red Room Academy with a poisonous spider species.

SET-10

1. Which monument complex includes the tomb of Iltutmish and the Ala'i-Darwaza?
   A. Purana Qila
   B. Qutb Minar
   C. Fatehpur Sikri
   D. Red Fort

2. Who is the first cricketer to hit a six off the first ball of a Test match?
   A. Chris Gayle
   B. Shahid Afridi
   C. AB de Villiers
   D. Kevin Pietersen

3. Which animals are called 'ecosystem engineers' by ecologists?
   A. Squirrels
   B. Rabbits
   C. Beavers
   D. Ants

4. In Dandi, on the shore of which waterbody did Mahatma Gandhi break the Salt Law?

    A. The Bay of Bengal
    B. The Ganges
    C. The Arabian Sea
    D. The Narmada

5. Port of Spain is the chief port of which country?
    A. Spain
    B. Trinidad and Tobago
    C. Fiji
    D. Brazil

6. What was translated by Sri Aurobindo as *'I bow to thee, Mother!'*?
    A. *Jana Gana Mana*
    B. *Vande Mataram*
    C. *Saare Jahan Se Achcha*
    D. *Kadam Kadam Badhaye Ja*

7. Rosaki and Monukka are varieties of which dry fruit?
    A. Cashewnut
    B. Walnut
    C. Raisin
    D. Date

8. With which film did Farhan Akhtar make his debut as a director?
    A. *Rock On!*
    B. *Don 2*
    C. *Dil Chahta Hai*
    D. *Lakshya*

9. Of all the union territories in India, which has the highest literacy rate?
   A. Dadra and Nagar Haveli
   B. Lakshadweep
   C. Andaman and Nicobar Islands
   D. Puducherry

10. The most common field of research for Nobel Laureates in medicine is...
    A. Genetics
    B. Cell physiology
    C. Diabetes
    D. Cancer

11. Rollerball and Biro are types of...
    A. Pens
    B. Hats
    C. Skates
    D. Hairstyles

12. In the NATO phonetic alphabet, which word is used to represent the letter 'K'?
    A. Kyoto
    B. Kangaroo
    C. Kilo
    D. King

13. On Twitter, a tweet which was liked used to be initially represented by a star. What is the symbol used now?
    A. A smiley

    B. A thumbs up

    C. A heart

    D. A happy face emoji

14. Which book was written by its author 'to induce kindness, sympathy and an understanding of treatment of horses'?

    A. *Moby-Dick*

    B. *Heidi*

    C. *Huckleberry Finn*

    D. *Black Beauty*

15. Reita Faria was the first Indian to win...

    A. An individual gold at the Asian Games

    B. The Miss World competition

    C. An Academy Award

    D. The Arjuna Award

BUZZER

1. Which team won the final of the IPL in 2008?

2. The Oxford Dictionary describes which creature as 'a slow-moving Old World lizard...with ability to change colour'?

3. Mysore Pak and Dharwad pedha are the popular sweet dishes of which Indian state?

4. Eddie Redmayne won the 2015 Oscar for potraying which scientist?

5. In India, which of these may act as proof of your identity: credit card or passport?

6. Who is the only living head of state to have served in World War II?

7. If you were visiting the Sea of Serenity or the Sea of Tranquility, where would you be?

8. Who wrote the novel *The Silkworm* under a pen name?

TAKE YOUR PICK

1. In 1878, which scientist coined the name Invention Factory for his research laboratory in a small village in New Jersey, USA?
    A. Thomas Alva Edison
    B. Alexander Graham Bell
    C. J.L. Baird
    D. Guglielmo Marconi

2. If a couple are celebrating their diamond jubilee, they have been married for how many years?
    A. 25
    B. 50
    C. 60
    D. 80

3. Which of these words comes from a Latin word which means 'something given'?
    A. Console
    B. Data
    C. Formulae
    D. Byte

4. What is the national reptile of Pakistan?
   A. Reticulated python
   B. Box turtle
   C. Indus crocodile
   D. Parson's chameleon

5. Which landmark in New Delhi, designed by Fariborz Sahba, has twenty-seven marble petals?
   A. Lotus Temple or Bahá'í House of Worship
   B. Akshardham temple
   C. Supreme Court of India
   D. Parliament building

6. Who is the first Indian to win the ICC ODI Player of the Year award twice?
   A. Virat Kohli
   B. Sachin Tendulkar
   C. M.S. Dhoni
   D. Virender Sehwag

7. On the morning of 6 April 1930, Mahatma Gandhi and his followers reached...
   A. Champaran
   B. Dandi
   C. Noakhali
   D. Madurai

8. Cox's Bazar, the longest uninterrupted natural beach in the world, is located in which country?
   A. Sri Lanka
   B. Nepal

C. Bhutan

D. Bangladesh

9. Which fictitional character said, "I have taken a loathing to wayfare, and when I hear the words 'Voyage' or 'Travel,' my limbs tremble"?
   A. Ali Baba
   B. Sinbad
   C. Aladdin
   D. Mir Kasim

10. Which chief minister was awarded the Ramon Magsaysay Award for Emergent Leadership in 2006?
    A. Akhilesh Yadav
    B. Arvind Kejriwal
    C. Omar Abdullah
    D. Naveen Patnaik

11. The Spanish gave this fruit a name which means 'monkey face', because the three eyes on it resemble the head and face of a monkey. Which fruit is it?
    A. Watermelon
    B. Coconut
    C. Guava
    D. Custard apple

12. Which of these is a type of bag?
    A. Brake
    B. Clutch
    C. Accelerator
    D. Carburettor

13. Ronald Lee Herrick gave it. His brother received it. And lead surgeon Dr Joseph Murray benefitted from it and went on to win the Nobel Prize. What are we talking about?
    A. Heart
    B. Kidney
    C. Liver
    D. Lung

14. In Hindu mythology, which flower does Saraswati sit on?
    A. Marigold
    B. Sunflower
    C. Lotus
    D. Rose

15. Which state has the most number of districts in India?
    A. Maharashtra
    B. Andhra Pradesh
    C. Arunachal Pradesh
    D. Uttar Pradesh

BUZZER

1. Who played the title role in the film *Bobby Jasoos*?
2. Who presented the union budget of India in 2016?
3. Which Bharat Ratna awardee was often referred to as Madiba?
4. Starfish have the most developed brains among all invertebrates: true or false?
5. In terms of area, which is the largest country situated

entirely in Asia?

6. In 2015, who became the first Indian batsman to score a century in a World Cup match against Pakistan?

7. Lahori Gate is the main entrance to which UNESCO World Heritage Site?

8. Which six-letter word is used to describe each of the four hindmost molars which appear in humans at the age of twenty?

SET-12

TAKE YOUR PICK

1. Which of these elements is named after a country?
   A. Indium
   B. Francium
   C. Tantalum
   D. Berkelium

2. Which famous temple is located on Venkatachala Hill?
   A. Tirumala Tirupati Temple
   B. Meenakshi Temple
   C. Golden Temple
   D. Kamakhya Temple

3. According to legend, the last few members of which of these are thought to have been hunted by the Maharaja of Surguja in 1947?
   A. Sangai
   B. Hangul
   C. Cheetah
   D. Nilgai

4. Colón, the currency of Costa Rica, is named after the Spanish name of...

    A. Christopher Columbus
    B. Santa Claus
    C. Nicolaus Copernicus
    D. Vasco da Gama

5. The three words, Citius-Altius-Fortius, in the Olympic motto mean...
    A. Faster - Higher - Stronger
    B. Ready - Steady - Go
    C. Industry - Impartiality - Integrity
    D. High - Higher - Highest

6. What does 'D' in the DSLR camera stand for?
    A. Digital
    B. Display
    C. Double
    D. Dolby

7. The Trimurti sculpture of which UNESCO World Heritage Site is a part of the logo of the Maharashtra Tourism Department?
    A. Ellora Caves
    B. Ajanta Caves
    C. Elephanta Caves
    D. Bhimbetka Rock Shelters

8. Which of these countries has a 0-km land boundary?
    A. Myanmar
    B. Japan
    C. Thailand
    D. Cambodia

9. "Oh, you can't help that," said the cat. "We're all mad here," is a quote from which novel?
   A. *Alice's Adventures in Wonderland*
   B. *Animal Farm*
   C. *Black Beauty*
   D. *Moby-Dick*

10. Zakir Hussain held it from 1967–69, V.V. Giri from 1969–74 and F.A. Ahmed from 1974–77. Which position am I talking about?
    A. President of India
    B. Governor of RBI
    C. Chief Justice of the Supreme Court of India
    D. Speaker of the Lok Sabha

11. The ancient Greeks helped introduce which device into Europe as sunshades?
    A. Umbrellas
    B. Hats
    C. Scarves
    D. Handkerchiefs

12. Lal Ambri and Sunehri are varieties of which fruit in India?
    A. Apple
    B. Pomegranate
    C. Grapes
    D. Guava

13. In which cartoon series would you come across a a small town named Furfuri Nagariya?

A. *Motu Patlu*
B. *Chhota Bheem*
C. *Mighty Raju*
D. *Chacha Bhatija*

14. Which of the following diseases is not caused by mosquito bites?
    A. Chikungunya
    B. Malaria
    C. Chicken Pox
    D. Dengue

15. Krishnattam is the folk theatre of...
    A. Odisha
    B. Kerala
    C. Uttar Pradesh
    D. Gujarat

BUZZER

1. Which continent is home to the longest river and largest desert in the world?
2. Who played the female lead in the film *2 States*?
3. According to the Gregorian calendar, if Christmas is on a Tuesday, what day would the following New Year day be?
4. *The Birth of Khadi* and *Indian Opinion* are two chapters from whose autobiography?
5. The saltwater species of which animal is the largest reptile in the world?
6. Sericin is a major component of wool, cotton or silk?

7. According to the Laws of Cricket, what has 'a face, a back, a toe, sides and shoulders'?
8. Which operating system is named after Linus Benedict Torvalds?

SET-13

TAKE YOUR PICK

1. Which of these words is common to a pair of deep-bodied drums and an African antelope?
    A. Dingo
    B. Dhole
    C. Bongo
    D. Sangai

2. Other than Mercury, which is the only planet with no moon?
    A. Venus
    B. Uranus
    C. Neptune
    D. Saturn

3. In which UNESCO World Heritage Site would you find the Kapali Yantra, Chakra Yantra and Rashi Valaya Yantra?
    A. Jantar Mantar
    B. Qutb Minar
    C. Rani Ki Vav
    D. Sun Temple, Konarak

4. A British surveyor, Sir Andrew Scott Waugh, gave

what its English name in 1865?
A. Platypus
B. Mount Everest
C. Sri Lanka
D. Dog Star

5. The creator of which video game was inspired by a late-night advertisement on kitchen knives?
   A. Candy Crush
   B. Temple Run
   C. Fruit Ninja
   D. Splatoon

6. If you saw a Grīvy's stallion, you would have seen a species of ...
   A. Tiger
   B. Camel
   C. Giraffe
   D. Zebra

7. Something of national importance is preserved in the Sarnath Museum near Varanasi in Uttar Pradesh. What is it?
   A. The first coin issued in independent India
   B. The State Emblem of India
   C. The original copy of the Constitution of India
   D. The first national flag of India

8. According to the Oxford English dictionary, what does 'autocorrect' in mobile phones correct?
   A. The quality of the clicked pictures

B. Incorrect spellings and grammar
C. Network issues
D. Date and time

9. Chitrakoot Parvat Mala, which includes Hanumaan Dhara, Janki Kund, Lakshman Pahari, is spread over Madhya Pradesh and...
   A. Maharashtra
   B. Odisha
   C. Uttar Pradesh
   D. Tamil Nadu

10. *Travels Into Several Remote Nations Of The World* is part of the original title of which book?
    A. *Gulliver's Travels*
    B. *Around the World in 80 Days*
    C. *Journey to the Center of the Earth*
    D. *Chitty Chitty Bang Bang*

11. Complete this quote by A.P.J. Abdul Kalam: 'It was an _____ mind asking me why India can't become a developed nation before 2020.'
    A. Alert
    B. Intelligent
    C. Ignited
    D. Inquisitive

12. What are Indian basil leaves commonly known as in Hindi?
    A. Tulsi
    B. Pudina

C. Dhania
D. Methi

13. Which article of clothing shares its name with a group of small islands situated about 1,050 km east of Cape Hatteras in USA?
   A. Capri pants
   B. Dungarees
   C. Bermuda shorts
   D. Poncho

14. In India, whose birth anniversary is celebrated as Sadbhavna Diwas?
   A. Rajiv Gandhi
   B. Jawaharlal Nehru
   C. Lal Bahadur Shastri
   D. P.V. Narasimha Rao

15. Who told the story of his life in the book *The Race of My Life: An Autobiography*?
   A. P.T. Usha
   B. Usain Bolt
   C. Milkha Singh
   D. Jesse Owens

BUZZER

1. The springbok is a national symbol of which country: South Africa or New Zealand?
2. The 2009 film *Harishchandrachi Factory* revolves around which iconic Indian?

3. Which game in India is said to have got its name from a Tamil word which means 'holding hands': kho kho, hockey or kabbadi?

4. Cloud to ground, sheet and spider are different types of which natural phenomenon: Lunar eclipse, lightning or tornado?

5. Which animal appeared on the standard flag of the last king of Sri Lanka?

6. In which state would you see the Group of Monuments at Mamallapuram?

7. Which superhero is also called the Dark Knight?

8. The word 'auditory' is associated with which sense: hearing or smelling?

SET-14

1. Who played the role of a young Preity Zinta in the Akshay Kumar and Preity Zinta- starrer *Sangharsh*?
   A. Sonam Kapoor
   B. Sonakshi Sinha
   C. Alia Bhatt
   D. Kareena Kapoor

2. The Natyanjali Dance Festival in Tamil Nadu pays a special tribute to which god?
   A. Brahma
   B. Vishnu
   C. Shiva
   D. Indra

3. What do the names of the two satellites of Mars—Phobos and Deimos—mean in English?
   A. Pride and Prejudice
   B. Fear and Panic
   C. Beauty and Perfection
   D. War and Peace

4. Who has written the book *Directions for Cooking by Troops, in Camp and Hospital*?

A. Joan of Arc
B. Mother Teresa
C. Anne Frank
D. Florence Nightingale

5. The first two Greek letters gave which of the following words?
   A. Theatre
   B. Alphabet
   C. Abacus
   D. Delta

6. Which Indian batsman has the highest scores of 219 and 319 in ODIs and Tests, respectively?
   A. Sachin Tendulkar
   B. Rahul Dravid
   C. Virender Sehwag
   D. Yuvraj Singh

7. In which organ of the human body would you find the Kupffer cells?
   A. Kidney
   B. Heart
   C. Liver
   D. Lung

8. What was the value of the highest denomination note ever printed by the Reserve Bank of India?
   A. 10,000
   B. 20,000
   C. 50,000

D. 80,000

9. The smallest bat in the world is also known as the...
   A. Bumblebee Bat
   B. Hummingbird Bat
   C. Grasshopper Bat
   D. Termite Bat

10. Whose museum, having the official address 221b, is actually situated at 239 Baker Street?
    A. Sherlock Holmes
    B. Miss Marple
    C. Hercule Poirot
    D. Father Brown

11. Which Indian leader wrote *Beyond Survival: Emerging Dimensions of Indian Economy*?
    A. Pranab Mukherjee
    B. A.P.J. Abdul Kalam
    C. Arun Jaitley
    D. P. Chidambaram

12. In computers, what are Stuxnet, PoisonIvy and Zeus different types of?
    A. Viruses
    B. Fonts
    C. Operating Systems
    D. Printers

13. The branches of which tree signify peace on the UN emblem?

A. Olive
B. Mango
C. Eucalyptus
D. Banyan

14. In which Indian city would you see the zero-mile marker, indicating the country's geographical centre?
    A. Gwalior
    B. Nagpur
    C. Raipur
    D. Dehra Dun

15. In the *Mahabharata*, who was Nakula's mother?
    A. Madri
    B. Kunti
    C. Draupadi
    D. Gandhari

BUZZER

1. Across which river is the Nagarjuna Sagar Dam built?
2. Connect the sixteenth letter of the Greek alphabet and a part of the name of a novel by Yann Martel.
3. Who is the first Indian woman to win an Olympic medal in boxing?
4. Complete the title of the book: *Five Point Someone: What Not To Do at* _____. *IIT/IIM/NDA*
5. Who was the president of the French Academy of Sciences from 1801–14?
6. What does the 'M' in M.S. Subbulakshmi stand for: Madurai or Mumbai?

7. What is obtained by grating the flesh of the fruit of the tree *Cocos nucifera* L.: coconut milk or ginger paste?
8. _____ Messaging Service. Fill in the blank to expand the abbreviation MMS.

SET-15

TAKE YOUR PICK

1. Name the duo who developed a concept called 'wing warping' while working on their famous creation.
    A. Wright Brothers
    B. Brothers Grimm
    C. Lumière Brothers
    D. Marx Brothers

2. Stephen Hillenburg combined his interests in marine biology and animation to create which character?
    A. Spongebob Squarepants
    B. The Octonauts
    C. PAW Patrol
    D. Shaun the Sheep

3. Which of these terms was born out of a competition announced by Mahatma Gandhi in the newspaper *Indian Opinion*?
    A. Khadi
    B. Satyagraha
    C. Ahimsa
    D. Charkha

4. Who has scored a record 18,426 runs in his ODI career?

A. Ricky Ponting
B. Sanath Jayasuriya
C. Sachin Tendulkar
D. Inzamam-ul-Haq

5. At royal functions in Australia, the national anthem of which country is played in addition to 'Advance Australia Fair'?
A. UK
B. USA
C. The Netherlands
D. Spain

6. Who was the first American president to win the Nobel Peace Prize?
A. Theodore Roosevelt
B. John F. Kennedy
C. Jimmy Carter
D. Barack Obama

7. *Pygoscelis antarcticus* is the scientific name of which animal species?
A. Walrus
B. Penguin
C. Polar bear
D. Seal

8. The title of the Chinese version of which book translates as *Foggy City Orphan*?
A. *Oliver Twist*
B. *Tale of Two Cities*

C. *Great Expectations*
D. *The Adventures of Tom Sawyer*

9. Which of these states in India was referred to as Pentapotamia by Greeks?
   A. West Bengal
   B. Tamil Nadu
   C. Punjab
   D. Odisha

10. What, of national importance to India, was created in two years, eleven months and seventeen days?
    A. The Parliament House
    B. The Constitution of India
    C. The national flag of India
    D. The Supreme Court of India

11. In computers, if U and I in the abbreviation GUI stand for user and interface, what does G stand for?
    A. Graphical
    B. Graded
    C. Gigabyte
    D. Grand

12. Which of these is named after its inventor?
    A. Saxophone
    B. Xylophone
    C. Harmonica
    D. Trumpet

13. In the *Mahabharata*, whose sons came to be known as Kauravas?
    A. Pandu
    B. Dhritarashtra
    C. Sri Krishna
    D. Shantanu

14. In the Gregorian calendar, how many months of the year begin with the letter 'J'?
    A. 3
    B. 4
    C. 5
    D. 6

15. Which actress plays the role of Alex Parrish in the ongoing TV show *Quantico*?
    A. Sushmita Sen
    B. Priyanka Chopra
    C. Aishwarya Rai
    D. Freida Pinto

BUZZER

1. The Rajaji National Park in Uttarakhand is named after C. Rajagopalachari or Rajendra Prasad?
2. In ancient Olympic Games, the wreath of which tree was placed on the winner's head at the official award ceremony?
3. Which state in India has the largest tea-growing area in India, with over 600 tea estates?
4. In the abbreviation DIY if D stands for Do, I stands

for It, then what does Y stand for?

5. The sign 'ampersand' stands for which conjunction?

6. In cartoons, who is Ninja Hattori's friend: Kenichi, Nobita or Shin Chan?

7. In which month is Universal Children's Day celebrated by the UN?

8. Sleepy, Dopey, Doc, Sneezy, Grumpy, Bashful and Happy are some of the characters from which 1937 Disney film?

SET-16

1. If you were visiting the Shakya Tank and the Maya Devi Temple in the Rupandehi district of Nepal, whose birthplace would you be visiting?
   A. Mahavira
   B. Buddha
   C. Guru Nanak
   D. Zoroaster

2. Amar, Gaminee and Suranjeevi are different forms of which sport?
   A. Kho Kho
   B. Kabaddi
   C. Asol Aap
   D. Mallakhamb

3. If a person received a Swarn Kamal (Golden Lotus), a cash prize worth ₹10 lakh and a shawl, which prestigious award would he be receiving?
   A. Arjuna Award
   B. Dadasaheb Phalke Award
   C. Jnanpith Award
   D. Bharat Ratna

4. In a June 2015 report of the World Economic Forum, which Indian organization was the eighth-largest employer in the world?
    A. India Post
    B. Indian Railways
    C. NTPC
    D. Indian Oil Corporation

5. In 1922, the telephone service in the USA was silenced for a minute to mark the funeral of...
    A. Alexander Graham Bell
    B. Thomas Alva Edison
    C. Humphry Davy
    D. Nikola Tesla

6. Which country awards the National Malala Peace Prize?
    A. Bangladesh
    B. Pakistan
    C. UK
    D. India

7. The Portuguese Man of War is a/the ...
    A. Submarine
    B. Marine animal
    C. Satellite of Mars
    D. Nickname of the football team of Portugal

8. In *Animal Farm*, what kind of creatures were Minimus, Snowball, Squealer and Napoleon?
    A. Horses

B. Pigs
C. Dogs
D. Donkeys

9. In India, Raja, Rocket, Roarer and Ranee are...
   A. Locomotives that pulled the first train
   B. Parts of the Jog Falls
   C. Character names in the film *Pink*
   D. Indian names of chess pieces

10. Which Indian wrote *Inspiring Thoughts*?
    A. Manmohan Singh
    B. Pranab Mukherjee
    C. A.P.J. Abdul Kalam
    D. Narendra Modi

11. Minty Meadow and Bubblegum Bridge are some of the levels in which video game?
    A. Fruit Ninja
    B. Angry Birds
    C. Candy Crush Saga
    D. Pac-Man

12. Ravana Chhaya, a form of puppetry, originated in which state of India?
    A. Manipur
    B. Odisha
    C. Gujarat
    D. Kerala

13. The fundus, the body, the antrum and the pylorus are the regions of which organ of the body?
    A. Kidney
    B. Liver
    C. Stomach
    D. Heart

14. Which Mughal emperor was named in honour of Sheikh Salim Chishti?
    A. Humayun
    B. Shah Jahan
    C. Jahangir
    D. Akbar

15. Coorg Honeydew and Surya are varieties of which fruit?
    A. Papaya
    B. Banana
    C. Orange
    D. Apple

BUZZER

1. In 1815, which leader briefly returned to power in his 'Hundred Days' campaign?
2. What has been called the 'Golden Fibre of Bangladesh': silk or jute?
3. Which superhero's original name is Tony Stark?
4. What does the 'G' in the colour scheme RGB stand for?

5. Who has been the longest-serving chief minister of Gujarat?
6. Female cassowaries are larger than males: true or false?
7. The name of which Indian state in the Northeast appears in the name of a classical dance form which originated there?
8. In the 1820s, the British started the commercial production of what when they planted a Chinese variety in Darjeeling?

SET-17

TAKE YOUR PICK

1. Shih Tzu, Lhasa Apso and Pekingese are breeds of which animal?
    A. Horse
    B. Camel
    C. Dog
    D. Sheep

2. If Gingka and Ryuga were using their beyblades, what would they be using?
    A. Spinning tops
    B. Kitchen knives
    C. Electric razors
    D. Tricycles

3. Fill in the blank to complete this quote by Mahatma Gandhi: 'An ounce of _____ is worth more than tons of preaching.'
    A. Practice
    B. Common sense
    C. Knowledge
    D. Patience

4. Which Indian actor played the role of Simon Masrani in the 2015 film *Jurassic World*?
   A. Naseeruddin Shah
   B. Irrfan Khan
   C. Anil Kapoor
   D. Anupam Kher

5. Which gemstone connects Cullinan, Hope and Excelsior?
   A. Ruby
   B. Jade
   C. Diamond
   D. Sapphire

6. Duty and Unity and Duty and Discipline were suggested as the motto of which organization?
   A. BSF
   B. CBI
   C. NCC
   D. RAF

7. In which month did the Constitution of India come into force?
   A. January
   B. August
   C. October
   D. December

8. Which of these is a city in south Goa?
   A. Christopher Columbus
   B. Marco Polo

    C. Vasco da Gama

    D. Ferdinand Magellan

9. Since the seventeenth century, which dance form has been associated with the Guruvayurappan Temple in Kerala, also known as Dwarka of South India?

    A. Krishnattam

    B. Kathakali

    C. Kuchipudi

    D. Kathak

10. Which of these is a photo-sharing site founded by Stewart Butterfield and Caterina Fake?

    A. Flickr

    B. Instagram

    C. Pinterest

    D. Picasa

11. In 1914, which famous scientist was appointed as director of the Kaiser Wilhelm Institute for Physics in Berlin?

    A. Albert Einstein

    B. Humphry Davy

    C. Louis Pasteur

    D. Julius Robert Oppenheimer

12. In the *Mahabharata*, who was the father of Ghatotkacha?

    A. Arjuna

    B. Bhima

    C. Nakula

    D. Sahadeva

13. In which month is International Women's Day celebrated by the UN?
    A. March
    B. April
    C. May
    D. June

14. What is the state animal of Manipur?
    A. Hangul
    B. Barasingha
    C. Sangai
    D. Nilgai

15. In which series of books would you come across the four Pevensie children, the White Witch and Aslan?
    A. *The Hunger Games*
    B. *The Chronicles of Narnia*
    C. *The Wizard of Oz*
    D. *Peter Pan*

BUZZER

1. In Rajasthan, dal and baati are usually eaten with churma or faluda?
2. Who played the female lead in the films *Chennai Express* and *Piku*?
3. Which character is believed to have been named in honour of the Nottingham cricketers Sherwin and Shacklock?
4. In terms of paper sizes, A4 is bigger than A3: serious or joking?

5. If you were in Assam, which of these would be nearer to you: Bay of Bengal or Arabian Sea?
6. Which dye, first derived from plants such as woad and dyer's knotweed, was most commonly applied to jeans?
7. In Indian awards, which word comes before Vibhushan, Bhushan and Shri?
8. In the 2015 ICC Cricket World Cup, the match between which two countries featured the national anthems written by the same person?

SET-18

TAKE YOUR PICK

1. According to a survey conducted by the London School of Marketing in 2015, who was the only Indian to appear on the list of the Top 20 Most Marketable Sports Stars in the World?
   A. M.S. Dhoni
   B. Sania Mirza
   C. Virat Kohli
   D. Saina Nehwal

2. What was acquired by Ranjit Singh from the Afghan ruler Shuja Shah Durrani as his price to support his return to power in Kabul?
   A. The Kohinoor
   B. Tipu Sultan's sword
   C. Red Fort
   D. The Indus River

3. According to an English idiom, what is mightier than a sword?
   A. Salt
   B. A spear
   C. A pen
   D. A shield

4. If the spice is called 'azafrán' in Spanish, then what is it called in Hindi?
   A. Adrakh
   B. Imli
   C. Kesar
   D. Jeera

5. The suit worn by which superhero, played by Robert Downey Jr, has about 450 pieces and weighs more than 40 kilograms?
   A. Superman
   B. Spiderman
   C. Iron Man
   D. Batman

6. What took place from 9 to 28 February in 1951 and 10 February to 1 March in 1961?
   A. The Census of India
   B. First Asian Games
   C. The First General Elections
   D. The Filmfare Awards

7. Which of these is located at the meeting point of the Bay of Bengal, the Indian Ocean and the Arabian Sea?
   A. Fatehpur Sikri
   B. Vivekananda Rock Memorial
   C. Gateway of India
   D. Elephanta Caves

8. African helmeted and Cantor's giant softshell are

different species of which of these reptiles?
A. Snail
B. Turtle
C. Snake
D. Chameleon

9. Wajid Ali Shah established the Lucknow gharana of which dance form?
A. Kathak
B. Kathakali
C. Manipuri
D. Bharatanatyam

10. In 1996, who resigned as the chief minister of Karnataka to be sworn in as the prime minister of India?
A. H.D. Deve Gowda
B. P.V. Narasimha Rao
C. Chandra Sekhar
D. I.K. Gujral

11. Which word means 'to scribble absent-mindedly'?
A. Adobe
B. Chrome
C. Doodle
D. Poke

12. Fill in the blank to complete this quote by Albert Einstein: 'The only source of knowledge is _____.'
A. Experience
B. Education

    C. Wealth

    D. Common sense

13. Zaire, Bundibugyo, Sudan, Taï Forest and Reston are the five subspecies of the virus of which disease?
    A. Malaria
    B. Ebola
    C. Dengue
    D. Chikungunya

14. In which month is World Environment Day celebrated by the UN?
    A. June
    B. July
    C. August
    D. September

15. The famous Bibi-ka-Maqbara was built by Prince Azam Shah in memory of his...
    A. Wife
    B. Sister
    C. Mother
    D. Daughter

BUZZER

1. The name of which card in India can be literally translated as 'foundation': PAN card or Aadhaar card?

2. Of the seven continents, which is the only continent larger than Africa, in terms of area?

3. Human beings can survive without one kidney: serious or joking?

4. 2006: Germany; 2010: South Africa; 2014: Brazil; 2018: _____.

5. An octopus has three hearts: serious or joking?

6. If Hyderabad is the capital of Andhra Pradesh, what is the capital of Telangana?

7. Whose statue at Pietermaritzburg Station marks the spot where he was thrown off a train?

8. While writing in English, which day of the week will have the most number of letters?

SET-19

TAKE YOUR PICK

1. On 14 July 2013, Rahul Gandhi became the last person to...
   A. Use a pager
   B. Use a diplomatic passport of India
   C. Receive a telegram message sent in India
   D. Create an account on Orkut

2. Which town in Virudhanagar district in Tamil Nadu is most famous for its fire-cracker industries?
   A. Vellore
   B. Sivakasi
   C. Tiruppur
   D. Salem

3. The recently discovered galaxy, Cosmos Redshift 7, has been nicknamed after which football player?
   A. Neymar Junior
   B. Lionel Messi
   C. Cristiano Ronaldo
   D. Wayne Rooney

4. The idea of which of these came from a statue which the creator called Egypt Brings Light to Asia?

A. Christ the Redeemer
B. Sphinx
C. The Statue of Liberty
D. The Merlion of Singapore

5. In the *Mahabharata*, what art did Eklavya teach himself by practising in front of a statue of Guru Dronacharya?
A. Mace fighting
B. Sword fighting
C. Archery
D. Swimming

6. What is the planting of new forests on lands that historically have not contained forests called?
A. Reforestation
B. Afforestation
C. Deforestation
D. Preforestation

7. Which colour is common to the flags of Thailand, Vietnam and Indonesia?
A. Red
B. Green
C. Orange
D. Yellow

8. In which language did Vishnu Sharma write the *Panchatantra*?
A. Hindi
B. Sanskrit

C. Pali

D. Tamil

9. In which ocean would you find the Great Barrier Reef, the largest living structure on Earth?
   A. Pacific Ocean
   B. Atlantic Ocean
   C. Indian Ocean
   D. Arctic Ocean

10. Which is the tallest bird native to Australia?
    A. Ostrich
    B. Emu
    C. Sarus Crane
    D. Greater Flamingo

11. Which director was born as Shankupani Sundaram?
    A. Mani Ratnam
    B. Prabhu Deva
    C. Priyadarshan
    D. Kamal Haasan

12. In *Spongebob Squarepants*, what kind of a creature is Patrick?
    A. Starfish
    B. Jellyfish
    C. Octopus
    D. Turtle

13. In a year, the Bharat Ratna can be awarded to a maximum of how many people?

A. Two
B. Three
C. Any number
D. Four

14. Powada is the traditional folk art from...
    A. Kerala
    B. Maharashtra
    C. Tamil Nadu
    D. Gujarat

15. In 2015, Neela Vaswani won the Grammy for Best Children's Album. Whose memoir did she narrate?
    A. Anne Frank
    B. Malala Yousafzai
    C. Enid Blyton
    D. Miley Cyrus

BUZZER

1. 'What is red, is a planet and is the focus of my orbit?' was the first tweet from Mangalyaan or Chandrayaan?
2. Mountain gorillas can climb trees: serious or joking?
3. In Indian Railways, ASR is the station code of which city?
4. The name of which trophy comes from a mock obituary notice written by S. Brooks and published in the *Sporting Times*?
5. Which is the second-driest continent on Earth?
6. The family of which evergreen tree is named so because each leaf resembles a spread hand?

7. Which duo starred in *Puss Gets The Boot* as Jasper the cat and Jinx the mouse?
8. Which ruler introduced copper coins with Gurumukhi legends?

SET-20

1. Which creature, also known as the nightcrawler, has ring-like segments called annuli?
    A. Jellyfish
    B. Salamander
    C. Earthworm
    D. Tarantula

2. In whose honour did Ravi Shankar create the raga Mohan Kauns?
    A. Lord Krishna
    B. Himself
    C. Mahatma Gandhi
    D. Dhyan Chand

3. Which of these states does not share its border with Bangladesh?
    A. Tripura
    B. Meghalaya
    C. Nagaland
    D. Mizoram

4. The former prime ministers P.V. Narasimha Rao, H.D. Deve Gowda and V.P. Singh also served as...

    A. RBI governors
    B. Lok Sabha speakers
    C. Chief ministers
    D. Lawyers by profession

5. Actor Saif Ali Khan's grandfather, Iftikhar Ali Khan, played Test cricket for...
    A. India and England
    B. India and Pakistan
    C. Pakistan and England
    D. Pakistan, England and India

6. In India, the first design of what was attempted by Colonel Forbes of the Calcutta Mint?
    A. The one-rupee note
    B. The national emblem
    C. India postage stamp
    D. The national flag

7. In the film *Tamasha,* where do Deepika Padukone and Ranbir Kapoor meet for the first time?
    A. Sicily
    B. Corsica
    C. Greenland
    D. Mauritius

8. Which symbol appeared on the tricolour when it was adopted as the national flag in 1931?
    A. The spinning wheel
    B. The lotus
    C. The tiger

D. The sun

9. If you were on Venus, you would see the sun rising from which direction?
   A. North
   B. South
   C. West
   D. East

10. A person's eye colour depends on the pigmentation of which structure?
    A. Retina
    B. Iris
    C. Pupil
    D. Cornea

11. The majority of the stories in the *Hitopadesha* have been taken from which of these works?
    A. *Panchatantra*
    B. *Natya Shastra*
    C. *Jataka Tales*
    D. *Sur Sagar*

12. What do Amit, Himanshu, Rahul, Tuheen and Nikhil call their band?
    A. Silk Route
    B. Indian Ocean
    C. Euphoria
    D. Aasma

13. Complete the name of a famous person: Mangte Chungneijang _____ ____.
    A. Jackie Chan
    B. Mary Kom
    C. Baichung Bhutia
    D. Aung San Suu Kyi

14. In comics, which superhero received the Super Soldier Serum?
    A. The Hulk
    B. Captain America
    C. Thor
    D. Iron Man

15. In Hindu mythology, who was the eighth child of Vasudeva and Devaki?
    A. Rama
    B. Krishna
    C. Bhishma
    D. Balarama

BUZZER

1. Connect: 120 feet, 12 seconds, 10:35 a.m., Kitty Hawk
2. Akbar offered Guru Amar Das gold coins to support the kitchen of which religious place?
3. About whom did Matthew Hayden say, 'I have seen God, he bats at number 4 for India.'?
4. The UN proclaimed 21 June as the International Day of...
5. In which book would you meet D'Artagnan, Aramis

and Porthos?

6. Who directed the 2014 film *Happy New Year*?
7. Ground kangaroos cannot walk backwards: true or false?
8. The first scientific expedition to measure the circumference of Earth was based in which country?

ANSWERS

SET-1

TAKE YOUR PICK

1. Tiger
2. TYPEWRITER
3. Purana Qila
4. Charles Dickens
5. Tuxedos
6. Greece
7. Ears
8. Tropical cyclones
9. UN headquaters
10. Saffron
11. 100
12. The Adventures of Tintin
13. A.R. Rahman
14. Maharashtra
15. Jnanpith Award

BUZZER

1. Charminar. Taj Mahal: 1631–48, Charminar: 1589–91
2. Koala
3. The Moon
4. Lakshadweep

5. Malgudi (found in the literary works by R.K. Narayan)
6. Mumbai Indians
7. Phone
8. Akbar

SET-2

TAKE YOUR PICK

1. Queen
2. The last British troops to leave independent India
3. Muslin
4. Native country
5. Motu
6. Gujarat Lions
7. Heart
8. Julius Caesar
9. Heart
10. Eggplant
11. Red Sea
12. Sumitra
13. The Indian Army
14. Rudyard Kipling (Rudyard was sent to England for schooling and it was there he met Wolcott Balestier, an American publisher and writer. They jointly wrote *Naulahka, A Novel of East and West*, the story of a priceless Indian jewel.)
15. West Bengal

BUZZER

1. False.They are arachnids. Arachnids have eight walking legs and insects have six walking legs.
2. Andhra Pradesh
3. Joking. It runs between Katra and Chennai.
4. Muga silk
5. Anne Frank
6. Sikhism
7. Kabaddi
8. Stomach

SET-3

TAKE YOUR PICK

1. Oxygen
2. Germany
3. India
4. Red Fort
5. *Alice's Adventures in Wonderland*
6. Stamps
7. Samosas
8. @
9. Diamond
10. Madhya Pradesh
11. Pepper
12. Palazzo
13. Bones
14. *The Lion King*
15. 21

BUZZER

1. Nepal
2. Herbivores
3. Doraemon
4. China
5. Arunachal Pradesh has sixteen letters, Jammu and Kashmir has fifteen letters.
6. Pitch
7. Jahangir
8. Jodhpur

SET-4

TAKE YOUR PICK

1. Teeth
2. First flight by man (Wilbur and Orville Wright's first flight on 17 December 1903)
3. Kapil Sibal
4. Great Barrier Reef
5. Butterfly
6. Climb Mount Everest
7. Vishwanathan Anand. It was renamed in 2015. The name of the minor planet is Vishyanand
8. Ping
9. Uttar Pradesh
10. C.V. Raman
11. William Shakespeare
12. Pungency in garlic and onions. Peeling onions makes you cry because they contain pyruvic acid, which is

released when an onion is cut.

13. Henna
14. Ebola
15. Delhi

BUZZER

1. Five
2. *NH10*
3. Mount Fuji
4. Hawa Mahal
5. Serious
6. Bihar
7. Space
8. Munshi Premchand

SET-5

TAKE YOUR PICK

1. Albert Einstein
2. Mother Teresa
3. Red panda
4. Economics. It has been awarded 47 times.
5. Brazil
6. A balance
7. *Angry Birds*
8. Caspian Sea
9. *Cinderella*
10. The President of India
11. Vermicelli

12. Ajanta Caves
13. Smallpox
14. Bal Gangadhar Tilak
15. Janak

BUZZER

1. Madhya Pradesh
2. Jalebi
3. Jhansi
4. Bark
5. Shuttlecock
6. Mouse
7. Neck
8. June

SET-6

TAKE YOUR PICK

1. Hawa Mahal
2. Indonesia
3. Sachin Tendulkar
4. Corridor
5. Goa
6. Eggs
7. *Baahubali*
8. Tears of joy
9. C.V. Raman
10. Shoes
11. Smell

12. Lamp inside a pot
13. 40,000
14. Fruit growing
15. A.P.J. Abdul Kalam

BUZZER

1. Chilli
2. Joking. As of July 2016, the population of Bangladesh is 15,61,86,882, while that of Russia is 14,23,55,415.
3. Saina Nehwal
4. China
5. False. They speak Dutch, French and German.
6. *Dhoom 3*
7. Gwalior
8. Fourteen

SET-7

TAKE YOUR PICK

1. Novak Djokovic
2. Mount Everest
3. Adolf Hitler
4. Wing-foot
5. Onions
6. *Star Wars*
7. Loudspeakers
8. Salt
9. Bhojpuri. The list has twenty-two languages.
10. The Dandi March

11. Muga silk
12. *Swami and Friends*
13. The tabla
14. Holmium
15. Pranab Mukherjee

BUZZER

1. K2/Mount Godwin Austen
2. Defence
3. South Africa
4. Water
5. Kryptonite
6. Katy Perry
7. Tuesday
8. Cactus

SET-8

TAKE YOUR PICK

1. Tipu Sultan
2. The cheetah
3. Usain Bolt
4. Equator
5. The Charminar
6. The elephant
7. Eyeglasses
8. *The Jungle Book*
9. Shawarma
10. Coins

11. Galileo Galilei
12. The Budget Session
13. Krishna
14. Swine Flu
15. Peshwa Bajirao

BUZZER

1. Rajasthan
2. Kidney
3. Sachin Tendulkar
4. True
5. Iris
6. Buddha
7. Chimpanzees
8. Atlantic

SET-9

TAKE YOUR PICK

1. Hyderabad
2. Pankaj and Shahid Kapur
3. Field hockey
4. Whale
5. Kanchenjunga
6. Taj Mahal
7. Socialist
8. Sugar
9. *Alice's Adventures in Wonderland*
10. The Prime Minister of India

11. Physics
12. Shoe
13. The lion
14. Hastinapura
15. Silver

BUZZER

1. Island
2. Mango
3. England
4. Salman Khan
5. Joking
6. A woman prime minister
7. Kerala
8. Black Widow

SET-10

TAKE YOUR PICK

1. Qutb Minar
2. Chris Gayle
3. Beavers
4. The Arabian Sea
5. Trinidad and Tobago
6. *Vande Mataram*
7. Raisin
8. *Dil Chahta Hai*
9. Lakshadweep
10. Genetics

11. Pens
12. Kilo
13. A heart
14. *Black Beauty*
15. The Miss World competition (in 1966).

BUZZER

1. Rajasthan Royals
2. Chameleon
3. Karnataka
4. Stephen Hawking
5. Passport
6. Queen Elizabeth II
7. The Moon
8. J.K. Rowling

SET-11

TAKE YOUR PICK

1. Thomas Alva Edison
2. 60
3. Data
4. Indus crocodile
5. Lotus Temple or Bahai House of Worship
6. M.S. Dhoni (in 2008 and 2009).
7. Dandi
8. Bangladesh
9. Sinbad
10. Arvind Kejriwal

11. Coconut. The word cocos means monkey-faced.
12. Clutch. It is a small flat bag without a handle.
13. Kidney
14. Lotus
15. Uttar Pradesh

BUZZER

1. Vidya Balan
2. Arun Jaitley
3. Nelson Mandela
4. False. They have no brains.
5. China
6. Virat Kohli
7. Red Fort
8. Wisdom

SET-12

TAKE YOUR PICK

1. Francium
2. Tirumala Tirupati Temple
3. Cheetah
4. Christopher Columbus
5. Faster - Higher - Stronger
6. Digital
7. Elephanta Caves
8. Japan
9. *Alice's Adventures in Wonderland*
10. President of India

11. Umbrellas
12. Apple
13. *Motu Patlu*
14. Chicken Pox
15. Kerala

BUZZER

1. Africa. The Nile River is the longest river in the world with a total length of 6,650 km. The Sahara is the largest desert in the world and is bigger than continental USA.
2. Alia Bhatt
3. Tuesday
4. Mahatma Gandhi. (Book: *The Story of My Experiments with Truth*)
5. Crocodile
6. Silk
7. Bat or blade of a bat
8. Linux

SET-13

TAKE YOUR PICK

1. Bongo
2. Venus
3. Jantar Mantar
4. Mount Everest
5. Fruit Ninja
6. Zebra

7. The State Emblem of India
8. Incorrect spellings and grammar
9. Uttar Pradesh
10. *Gulliver's Travels*
11. Ignited
12. Tulsi
13. Bermuda shorts
14. Rajiv Gandhi
15. Milkha Singh

BUZZER

1. South Africa
2. Dadasaheb Phalke
3. Kabaddi
4. Lightning
5. Lion
6. Tamil Nadu
7. Batman
8. Hearing

SET-14

TAKE YOUR PICK

1. Alia Bhatt
2. Shiva
3. Fear and Panic
4. Florence Nightingale
5. Alphabet
6. Virender Sehwag

7. Liver
8. 10,000
9. Bumblebee bat
10. Sherlock Holmes
11. Pranab Mukherjee
12. Viruses
13. Olive
14. Nagpur
15. Madri

BUZZER

1. Krishna
2. Pi
3. M.C. Mary Kom
4. IIT
5. Napoleon
6. Madurai.The name M.S. Subbalakshmi stands for Madurai Shanmukhavadivu Subbulakshmi.
7. Coconut milk
8. Multimedia

SET-15

TAKE YOUR PICK

1. Wright Brothers
2. Spongebob Squarepants
3. Satyagraha
4. Sachin Tendulkar
5. UK

6. Theodore Roosevelt
7. Penguin
8. *Oliver Twist*
9. Punjab
10. The Constitution of India
11. Graphical
12. Saxophone (from the name of Adolphe Sax).
13. Dhritarashtra
14. Three. January, June and July
15. Priyanka Chopra

BUZZER

1. C. Rajagopalachari. The national park is situated in Uttarakhand.
2. Olive, also known as 'kotinos' in Greek.
3. Assam
4. Yourself
5. And
6. Kenichi
7. November
8. *Snow White and the Seven Dwarfs*

SET-16

TAKE YOUR PICK

1. Buddha
2. Kabaddi
3. Dadasaheb Phalke Award. It is given to a film personality for his/her outstanding contribution to the

growth and development of Indian cinema.
4. Indian Railways
5. Alexander Graham Bell
6. Pakistan
7. Marine animal
8. Pigs
9. Parts of the Jog Falls
10. A.P.J. Abdul Kalam
11. Candy Crush Saga
12. Odisha
13. Stomach
14. Jahangir
15. Papaya

BUZZER

1. Napoleon Bonaparte
2. Jute
3. Iron Man
4. Green
5. Narendra Modi, from 2001 to 2014.
6. True
7. Manipur
8. Tea

SET-17

TAKE YOUR PICK

1. Dog
2. Spinning tops

3. Practice
4. Irrfan Khan
5. Diamond
6. NCC
7. January. It came into force on 26 January 1950.
8. Vasco da Gama
9. Krishnattam
10. Flickr
11. Albert Einstein
12. Bhima
13. March
14. Sangai
15. *The Chronicles of Narnia*

BUZZER

1. Churma
2. Deepika Padukone
3. Sherlock Holmes
4. Joking
5. Bay of Bengal
6. Indigo
7. Padma
8. India and Bangladesh

SET-18

TAKE YOUR PICK

1. M.S. Dhoni
2. The Kohinoor

3. A pen
4. Kesar
5. Iron Man
6. The Census of India
7. Vivekananda Rock Memorial
8. Turtle
9. Kathak
10. H.D. Deve Gowda
11. Doodle
12. Experience
13. Ebola
14. June
15. Mother

BUZZER

1. Aadhaar card
2. Asia
3. Serious
4. Russia, the host country of the FIFA World Cup.
5. Serious
6. Hyderabad
7. Mahatma Gandhi. It is a city in South Africa.
8. Wednesday

SET-19

TAKE YOUR PICK

1. Receive a telegram message sent in India
2. Sivakasi

3. Cristiano Ronaldo
4. Statue of Liberty
5. Archery
6. Afforestation
7. Red. Thailand: red, blue and white; Indonesia: red and white; Vietnam: red and yellow
8. Sanskrit
9. Pacific Ocean
10. Emu
11. Prabhu Deva
12. Starfish
13. Three
14. Maharashtra
15. Malala Yousafzai

BUZZER

1. Mangalyaan. It was India's maiden mission to Mars.
2. Serious
3. Amritsar
4. Ashes
5. Australia
6. Palm
7. *Tom and Jerry*
8. Ranjit Singh

SET-20

TAKE YOUR PICK

1. Earthworm

2. Mahatma Gandhi
3. Nagaland
4. Chief Ministers. P.V. Narasimha Rao was the chief minister of Andhra Pradesh from 1971–73. H.D. Deve Gowda was the chief minister of Karnataka. V.P. Singh was the chief minister of Uttar Pradesh, 9 June 1980–28 June 1982.
5. India and England
6. India postage stamp
7. Corsica
8. The spinning wheel
9. West
10. Iris
11. *Panchatantra*
12. *Indian Ocean*
13. Mary Kom
14. Captain America
15. Krishna

BUZZER

1. The first flight by the Wright Brothers
2. Golden Temple
3. Sachin Tendulkar
4. Yoga
5. *The Three Muskeeters*
6. Farah Khan
7. True
8. Ecuador

www.ingramcontent.com/pod-product-compliance
Lightning Source LLC
Chambersburg PA
CBHW022152080426
42734CB00006B/410